The 25 Deadliest Animals in the World

25 Most Deadly Animals In The World That You Should Know! Incredible Facts & Images Of Some Of The Most Deadly Animals On The Planet

(Awesome Creature Series)

By Hathai Ross

Table of Contents

Introduction 5

Chapter One: Great White Shark 6

Chapter Two: Leopard 8

Chapter Three: Box Jellyfish 10

Chapter Four: Rhinoceros 12

Chapter Five: Brazilian Wandering Spider 14

Chapter Six: Lion 16

Chapter Seven: Komodo Dragon 18

Chapter Eight: Deathstalker 20

Chapter Nine: Hyena 22

Chapter Ten: Stonefish 25

Chapter Eleven: Saltwater Crocodile 27

Chapter Twelve: Boomslang 29

Chapter Thirteen: Cone Snail 32

Chapter Fourteen: Hippopotamus 34

Chapter Fifteen: Puffer Fish 36

Chapter Sixteen: Africanized Honey Bee 38

Chapter Seventeen: Black Mamba 40

Chapter Eighteen: Cape Buffalo..................................42

Chapter Nineteen: Carpet Viper.................................44

Chapter Twenty: Mosquito..46

Chapter Twenty-One: Polar Bear...............................48

Chapter Twenty-Two: Tsetse Fly................................50

Chapter Twenty-Three: African Elephant....................52

Chapter Twenty-Four: Poison Dart Frog.....................54

Chapter Twenty-Five: Blue-Ringed Octopus...............56

Conclusion..58

About the Author...59

Next Steps..60

Check Out My Other Books......................................61

Copyright: Published in the United States by
© Greenslopes Direct
Published October 2017

All rights reserved. No part of this publication may be reproduced, stored in retrieval system, copied in any form or by any means, electronic, mechanical, photocopying, recording or otherwise transmitted without written permission from the publisher. Please do not participate in or encourage piracy of this material in any way. You must not circulate this book in any format. Hathai Ross does not control or direct users' actions and is not responsible for the information or content shared, harm and/or actions of the book readers.

In accordance with the U.S. Copyright Act of 1976, the scanning, uploading and electronic sharing of any part of this book without the permission of the publisher constitute unlawful piracy and theft of the author's intellectual property. If you would like to use material from the book (other than just simply for reviewing the book), prior permission must be obtained by contacting the author at greenslopesdirect@gmail.com

Thank you for your support of the author's rights.

Introduction

Thank you for downloading this book.

Have you ever wondered which animals on this planet are the deadliest ?

Well, now are are moments away from finding out !

In this book. you will learn:

- Amazing facts about these deadly animals.
- How these animals survive.
- What they look like – in gorgeous pictures
- Where they live
- Why they are deadly
- And so much more

Read this book today and you will also learn a many things about these deadly creatures!

Chapter One: Great White Shark

If you have been wondering which animal should be declared the king of the ocean, then wonder no more. It's time to meet the deadliest of the deep-sea predators!

The great white shark is found in all the oceans of the world. This sea creature loves the cool waters that are near the coastline of every continent.

So why are they called "Great White?" These sharks may be grey in color, but the underside of their belly is usually white, hence the name. The great white shark is super-fast. It can swim at a speed of 60 kilometers an hour (37 miles per hour), thanks to its sleek shape and powerful tail.

Not only is the great white shark a very fast swimmer, but it is also the biggest predatory fish in the world. This means that no other animal or fish in the ocean hunts and eats the great white shark. These sharks usually grow to a length of 4.6 meters (13.8 feet), though some great whites reach a whopping 6 meters (18 feet). That is half the length of your school bus!

If you are unlucky enough to find yourself staring into the mouth of this beast, you will get an up-close look at 300 of the sharpest triangular teeth you've ever seen. Older sharks use their fearsome teeth to gobble up other sea mammals such as small whales, seals, and sea lions. Younger sharks usually eat smaller creatures such as rays and small fish.

Believe it or not, humans are not really part of their menu. While there have been reported cases of great whites attacking people, these are rare and random cases. Most researchers say that great white sharks only bite people because they are curious about humans, so that is definitely a relief.

Here's another amazing fact about these creatures. Apart from their fearsome bite, they also have an incredibly powerful sense of smell. If you were to place just one drop of your blood in 100 liters of water, a great white would still be able to find it! They use this unique ability to locate their prey from miles away. They swim underneath them and then burst upwards rapidly, catching them by surprise. When you see a great white shark jumping up out of the water with its mouth wide open, just know that some poor creature has just turned into a "great white lunch."

The great white shark has no natural enemies in the ocean and is the top of the food chain. Unfortunately, the only threat it has comes from illegal hunting and overfishing by humans. This deadly king of the ocean is slowly becoming an endangered species.

Chapter Two: Leopard

The leopard is one of the big jungle cats and is a close relative of the lion, jaguar, and tiger. If you want to see a leopard in its natural habitat, you will have to go to northeast Africa, sub-Saharan Africa, Central Asia, China, or India.

So why exactly should we fear the leopard? What's so special about this overgrown jungle cat?

Well, the first thing to know about leopards is that they are very silent hunters. You simply won't see a leopard attacking you until it's too late. Unlike other big cats that make a lot of noise and start chasing you from far, the leopard is a master of the element of surprise. This is why they often choose to hunt alone instead of in a pack.

If an animal is injured, they usually run away and hide. But the leopard is not like most animals. The worst thing you can do is to harm a leopard because that's when it displays just how dangerous it can be. If you thought the lion was more lethal to humans, then you were wrong. The leopard considers humans to be a better target. Leopards are even able to attack and kill gorillas in the wild, so humans aren't going to put up much of a fight.

The leopard is a skilled and robust hunter that comfortably hides in the trees and waits for its prey to pass by. Its spotted coat helps it to remain hidden from other animals until it's too late for them to run. The leopard then pounces on its prey and kills it by biting its skull or neck. The leopard is known for having a very powerful bite. Once bitten, you are highly likely to develop a nasty bacterial infection. It is believed that most of the human deaths caused by leopard attacks are a result of the bacterial infection rather than the injuries inflicted by the animal.

The leopard is strong enough to drag a large animal up a tree to keep its meal safe from scavengers like hyenas. Leopards have excellent night vision and can hunt well in the dark. This gives it a massive advantage against its prey. Most cats don't enjoy getting into any water, but the leopard loves swimming and can sometimes fish for crabs or fish when it needs to.

The average leopard weighs between 32 to 82 kilograms (70 to 180 pounds). They usually grow to between 1.3 to 1.9 meters (4 to 7 feet) in length and reach a height of 1.4 meters (4.5 feet).

The sad thing about this deadly cat is that their numbers are gradually reducing, especially those that live in Asia.

Chapter Three: Box Jellyfish

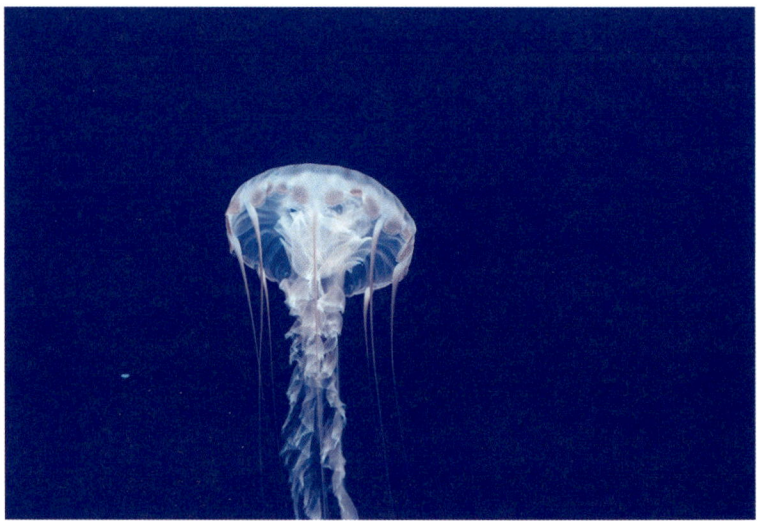

Though the box jellyfish may seem like a cute animal, you should be warned that touching one of these creatures is a very bad move. The box jellyfish is found in the warm coastal waters of the Indian and the Pacific Ocean, but the most dangerous types of box jellyfish live off the coast of Northern Australia.

The body shape of these creatures resembles a box-shaped bell the size of a basketball. It has about 60 tentacles that measure 5 meters (15 feet) in length. These tentacles are located at the corners of its body and are grouped into four clusters. Each tentacle is covered in small darts or stinging cells filled with poison. If anybody touches just 3 meters (9 feet) of its tentacles, they could die.

The moment the box jellyfish stings you with its tentacles, you immediately become paralyzed and suffer a heart attack. Animals that are injected with this poison usually die within a few minutes. In fact, the box jellyfish is said to cause more human deaths than crocodiles, sharks, and stonefish combined!

The good news is that though there are about 50 different types of box jellyfish, very few of them have the poison that can kill human beings. Box jellyfish don't target humans, and most of the cases of people getting stung are a result of snorkeling tourists touching its tentacles by accident.

The Australian box jellyfish wears the crown of the most lethal marine animal. It is larger than all the other box jellyfish and can grow to about 33 centimeters (1 foot) in diameter. It has thick tentacles that look like bootlaces, and these tentacles can grow up to 3 meters long. The body of a box jellyfish is transparent, which means you will stare right through it and not even know it is there. This makes it very hard to see when you are swimming underwater.

If you have ever observed how jellyfish move in the water, then you know that jellyfish simply float wherever the waves take them. Most jellyfish cannot control their direction of movement because they can't even see where they are going. However, the box jellyfish doesn't play by those rules. These deadly marine assassins can swim at a maximum speed of 7.4 kilometers an hour (4.6 miles per hour).

Box jellyfish also have very sophisticated eyes. They have four eyes that are located at the center of all sides of the box. This is bad news for its prey because its vision and speed give the box jellyfish the ability to chase down its prey. The box jellyfish usually target small fish and shrimp.

There is only one animal that jellyfish will do anything to avoid, and that is the turtle. For some reason, turtles just don't feel the sting of a jellyfish, and they just go ahead and make a meal them.

Chapter Four: Rhinoceros

It's humongous. It's ugly. It's faster than it looks. And it can easily flip over a car with people inside. We introduce to you: the rhinoceros.

Rhinos are commonly found in Africa and exist in two species, the black rhino and the white rhino. The black rhino weighs about 1400 kilograms (3080 pounds), and the white rhino weighs nearly twice that size. The confusing thing about their names is that rhinos are neither black nor white. They are actually grey in color.

However, there will be no confusion in recognizing a rhino when you see one. The large body, stumpy legs, and horns sticking out of the middle of its face are a dead giveaway. Rhinos are built like tanks. Their bodies appear to be covered in armor, and with their vast size, these animals can be quite intimidating.

One interesting thing about these large mammals is that they are known to have very poor eyesight. So, if this is true, why should you be afraid of an animal that can barely even see you?

Though their eyesight is terrible, a rhino can run pretty fast for an animal with such a large body. It may be easy to sneak up on a rhino, and it will definitely be startled to see you, but escaping from it will be a tough thing to do. Those stumpy legs can run at a speed of more than 50 kilometers an hour (40 miles per hour), and a rhino's horns can grow to a length of over one meter.

Now close your eyes and think of a one-meter horn stuck on a 1400 kilogram body charging at 50 kilometers an hour. What do you think would happen?

Once a rhino has you within its sight and feels threatened, it runs at you at full speed. It uses its large, tank-like body and horns as lethal weapons. Most people expect the horn to be the most dangerous weapon, but the rhino's most dangerous weapon is its speed and size. Once it starts charging, nothing can stand in its way. An angry rhino can slam into a vehicle and tip it over.

The rhino may have bad eyesight and a small brain, but its nasty temper and tendency to charge at everything that bothers it makes it a dangerous beast. On the other hand, this animal is quickly heading toward extinction thanks to poachers who kill it for its valuable horns.

Chapter Five: Brazilian Wandering Spider

Would you mess with a spider whose scientific name means "Murderess?" Neither would I!

This spider is found mainly in Brazil, and some species have also been found in other Latin American countries like Argentina and Costa Rica. It would have been great if the Brazilian Wandering Spider stayed in South America, but unfortunately, these spiders can travel across continents through banana shipments. When cargo ships transport bananas from Brazil to Europe and North America, some of these spiders hide in the bananas and end up in many different countries.

The Brazilian Wandering Spider has been topping the Guinness Book of World records for several years as the most venomous spider on the planet. The bite of this spider is enough to kill a human being, and children are most at risk.

These spiders are well-known for their aggressiveness. If they feel threatened, Brazilian Wandering Spiders lift their front four legs and expose the reddish hair that surrounds their fangs. If you see this happening, then it's time you beat a hasty retreat.

Once one of these spiders bite you, you will immediately experience symptoms such as sweating, extreme burning pain where you were bitten, and goosebumps. After 30 minutes, you will develop nausea, blurred vision, stomach cramps, vertigo, convulsions, and hypothermia. It is vital that you seek immediate medical attention.

So far, we know why they are called "Brazilian," but why are they referred to as "Wandering?" If you look around your house, you may notice a few cobwebs built by small spiders to trap their food. These webs tend to catch small insects like flies and so on. However, the Brazilian Wandering Spider doesn't waste time building a web and waiting for its prey to get trapped. It merely decides to wander through the forest floor and attack its prey directly!

Without a doubt, any spider that chooses to actively hunt for its food must be a mean killer. Brazilian Wandering Spiders spend their days hiding beneath logs and in holes. At night, they come out to attack or ambush their prey. They usually target other spiders, insects, small amphibians, and mice.

Any spider that can bring down a mouse must be quite large. Their bodies can grow to about 5 centimeters with a leg span of about 15 centimeters. Brazilian Wandering Spiders come in many different colors, though most of them are brown and have a black mark on their abdomen.

Chapter Six: Lion

There's a reason why the lion is called "the king of the jungle." These beasts are armed with speed, brute strength, agility, and sharp claws and teeth.

These big cats are found mainly in Africa, though there is a small population that can still be found in India. Lions are, therefore, divided into two subspecies – African and Asiatic lions.

The African lion is the largest carnivore on the continent and can grow to a length of up to 2 meters (6.5 feet), not including the tail. The African lion weighs between 120 to 191 kilograms (265 to 420 pounds). The Asiatic lion is usually much bigger and can grow to a length of 2.8 meters (9.2 feet). They weigh between 120 to 226 kilograms (300 to 500 pounds).

Lions are natural killers. They hunt and eat large animals such as antelopes, wildebeest, buffaloes, and zebras.

Sometimes a pride of lions will even take down a full-sized elephant. Lions will chase down their prey and use their mighty front paws to knock them over. They will then use their strong jaws and teeth to strangle the victim to death.

The female lions are the ones who do all the hunting. The females tend to form hunting groups that are very skilled at bringing down their prey. The first group chases down an animal in a specific direction while the second team lays an ambush for the prey. This superior hunting technique makes them very difficult to get away from. Lions are efficient hunters who rarely fail in bringing down their prey.

The male lions are considered the protectors of the pride. However, don't be fooled by the lazy appearance of the male lion. When it's time to fight, they can be extremely aggressive and deadly. In fact, apart from human beings, the only other animal that can attack a lion is a crocodile.

Lions have been known to attack people and cause between 100 to 300 deaths every year. With their enormous size and weight, these animals can easily take down a human being. However, most of the lions that consistently attack people are old, sick, or starving. When a lion is weak, it just finds it easier to hunt humans than chase down other faster animals.

Chapter Seven: Komodo Dragon

Imagine being chased down the street by a lizard; not by your regular house gecko or some tree lizard. This is an 8-foot, 200-pound lizard with a massive head, long claws, large tail, forked tongue, and ugly leathery skin.

The Komodo dragon is the biggest lizard alive today. They are found in their natural habitat in the islands of Indonesia, where the local people refer to them as "land crocodile."

So, what makes the Komodo dragon so deadly?

Komodo dragons are carnivorous creatures, and they feed on the flesh of large animals such as deer, water buffalo, pigs, and in some instances, humans. The Komodo may be a large and heavy animal, but it is still a reasonably fast runner. It can reach a speed of 20 kilometers per hour (13 miles per hour). If you think this is slow, then consider this. The speed of an average human is about 24 kilometers an hour (15 miles per hour)! This means that you would barely be able to escape a Komodo dragon if you somehow managed to sprint at your fastest speed.

But still, that isn't the Komodo's most lethal weapon. Deer and buffalo can easily leave a Komodo in the dust. The Komodo has developed a hunting technique based on stealth, smell, brute force, and poisonous saliva. The Komodo dragon uses its forked tongue to smell the air and detect the direction an animal is coming from. It then waits quietly, sometimes even for hours, until its prey crosses its path. The Komodo then jumps and knocks the animal over using its powerful front feet. It uses its sharp and jagged teeth to tear its prey apart – while the prey is still alive!

If the animal somehow manages to get up and escape, the Komodo doesn't have to chase it. It knows that its poisonous saliva will do the trick. The escaping prey will die of blood poisoning in less than 24 hours, and the Komodo will use its excellent sense of smell to track it down and feed on it. It is believed that the saliva of a Komodo dragon contains around 50 strains of bacteria.

Male Komodo dragons are generally larger than the females. Their skin comes in many different colors, including grey, green, orange, and blue. This skin is tough and is made up of bony plates.

Komodo dragons also have excellent eyesight and can see objects that are 300 meters (985 feet) away. Considering all the weapons that a Komodo has in its arsenal, we should all be grateful that this beast is only found in the remote islands of Indonesia.

Chapter Eight: Deathstalker

The deathstalker is a species that comes from the most feared and poisonous family of scorpions on the planet. The deathstalker can be found in most of the countries in the Middle East and North Africa. This scorpion prefers to live in dry areas like deserts and scrubland. If you want to see a deathstalker scorpion, then you would have to take a trip to the Arabian, Sahara, and Thar Deserts.

Since they live in extremely hot areas, deathstalkers tend to hide under rocks and debris during the day. They will also inhabit animal burrows that have been abandoned and sometimes dig their own holes about 20 centimeters below the surface. Deathstalkers have even been known to enter people's homes to get some shade from the hot sun. When the sun goes down, then the deathstalker comes out to play.

The deathstalker scorpion has a nasty and painful sting. It is an aggressive and fearsome animal that has very rare and extremely toxic venom. Its venom contains different kinds of toxins, and anything that is stung by a deathstalker soon suffers from convulsions, breathing problems, and heart failure. The makes the deathstalker's venom one of the most powerful of all scorpion species.

Though the sting of a deathstalker can be extremely painful, its venom doesn't usually kill people. That is if you are a healthy adult. Those who are most at risk of dying from a deathstalker sting include the elderly, people with heart conditions, and small children.

The deathstalker has large pincers which are not really that strong. However, it doesn't need to bite its prey very hard because it can simply sting and kill it with the potent venom in its tail.

Regarding size, the deathstalker grows to between 2.5 to 10 centimeters (1 to 4 inches) long. Since the female scorpions are the ones that must carry the young scorpions when they are born, they are usually much bigger than the males. The color of deathstalkers ranges from green to pale yellow. Their abdomens are traditionally marked with horizontal grey stripes.

It usually eats spiders, earthworms, centipedes, and other small insects. Researchers are studying the possibility of using the venom of the deathstalker to treat brain tumors or diabetes.

Chapter Nine: Hyena

The hyena may be well-known for its cackling laugh and odd-looking body, but don't let this fool you into thinking that this animal is a joke. Hyenas are powerful, dangerous, and can attack and kill much larger animals.

Hyenas are carnivorous animals that look like dogs. They are found in many parts of Africa as well as in Asia. Hyenas outnumber all the other large carnivores in Africa, and this means that they often encounter human beings.

For some reason, people have always thought that hyenas are timid and cowardly. However, the truth is that they are quite bold and dangerous. Hyenas are known to attack and kill livestock, which naturally creates conflict with humans. There are times when a pack of hyenas will also attack humans, and children are especially at risk.

Though hyenas are known to be scavengers, they are also very skilled hunters. They are opportunists who are always looking for the easiest way to kill their prey. A hyena will chase after the calves of wildebeest or antelopes since they are easier to catch. When they scavenge for food, they simply wait until another animal has made the kill before they jump in as a pack and steal the meat. Most of the other carnivores in the African Savannah view the hyena as a pest because of this behavior.

The thing that makes the hyena dangerous is its powerful jaws. The hyena may have a small body, but its bite is stronger than that of many larger carnivores. A hyena can chew through bones, hooves, and according to some campers, even metallic pots and pans. The stomach of a hyena can digest practically anything it eats. This is why when a pack of hyenas starts eating an animal, they never leave anything behind except a patch of blood. The only parts of an animal that a hyena cannot digest are the hair, hooves, and horns. When it eats these parts, it later vomits them out in the form of pellets.

Hyenas are not just powerful. They are very intelligent and their brains can function like that of a primate or human being. This enables them to organize themselves into efficient hunting packs.

The hyena also has a strange-looking body. Its front legs are much longer than the hind legs, and it usually walks like a bear. The laughing sound that a hyena makes is used to tell other hyenas that there is some food nearby. They also communicate with each other using various signals and body postures. If a hyena carries its tail straight, that means it is about to attack. If the tail is upward and over its back, that means the hyena is very excited. However, if it tucks its tail between its legs, then it is afraid and will run away.

Animals that are likely to attack a hyena include lions and hunting dogs. Due to their tendency to attack people and livestock, the most significant threat to hyenas comes from humans.

Chapter Ten: Stonefish

When it comes to lethal sea creatures, size truly doesn't matter. Weighing in at 2 kilograms (5 pounds) and measuring a mere 30 centimeters, the stonefish holds the title for the deadliest (and probably ugliest!) fish on the planet.

Stonefish are found in the Indian and Pacific Oceans. A stonefish has a row of 13 spines on its back, each containing sacs filled with poison. However, this venom is not the biggest weapon that the stonefish has in its arsenal. The stonefish uses creative camouflage and lightning-bolt speed to hide and ambush its prey.

The stonefish hunts by lying down on the ocean floor or some coral. It can camouflage itself and look like a piece of rock. It then waits on the seabed for shrimp or small fish to swim by, and within 0.015 seconds, the attack is over! The stonefish pounces on its prey and sucks it into its hungry mouth. Its prey doesn't even realize what has happened until it is too late.

Its ability to disguise itself as a piece of beautiful and colorful coral makes it a threat to deep-sea divers. Most people who get stung by the stonefish either touch it or accidentally step on it. The stonefish doesn't use its poison to attack but rather as a defensive weapon. Since the venom is in its spines, it is only released when a predator applies pressure on its back. If a predator bites down on the stonefish, then the spines injure the predator, and the deadly venom travels up into the wound.

So, what do you do in case you are stung by a stonefish? The first thing to do is use hot water to provide some relief for the terrible pain. You should then seek immediate medical treatment and receive anti-venom. If you don't get treatment, then you will experience extreme pain, shock, temporary paralysis, and heart failure. Death occurs in less than an hour.

To prevent accidentally getting stung by stonefish when snorkeling or diving, it is recommended that you wear shoes with thick soles and step carefully on the seabed. If you jump on a stonefish, even the thick soles won't prevent the spines from penetrating the shoes. You should also be careful when touching objects that look like rocks.

One fact that most people don't know is that unlike most other fish, the stonefish can survive out of water for 24 hours!

Chapter Eleven: Saltwater Crocodile

The saltwater crocodile is the biggest reptile in the world. It is found mainly in the northern region of Australia and loves to inhabit slow-moving rivers along the coast.

The saltwater crocodile is a huge, ugly, and ferocious creature. It can grow to nearly 7 meters (25 feet) in length, and some of these animals weigh up to 2 tons. What makes it even more deadly is its extremely powerful bite. The saltwater crocodile has a bite pressure of 3,000 pounds per square inch. This is almost ten times more powerful than that of a great white shark.

Their eyes, nostrils, and ears are positioned very high on its head. This allows the saltwater crocodile to remain under the water with only its eyes, nose, and ears sticking out. When they detect their prey, they stay still and may even appear to be a log floating on the water. When the prey approaches, the saltwater crocodile lunges at it and grabs it using its powerful teeth. Instead of tearing the animal's flesh, the crocodile will drag it into the water. They roll around underwater with their victim until it drowns. Then they use their sharp teeth to tear the flesh apart.

If you thought this reptile is a slow-mo because of its size, think again. It can move through water at a speed of 27 kilometers per hour (18 miles per hour), which is way faster than the fastest Olympic swimmer. Though they may not be as fast on land, they are still able to cover several meters reasonably quickly and surprise their prey before it gets the chance to move.

Another reason why you need to fear the saltwater crocodile is that it will attack and eat a human if it gets the chance. Most of the animals in this book will only attack you as a means of defense, or to protect their territory. However, the saltwater crocodile doesn't need an excuse to attack. All it needs is an opportunity.

Sharks may only bite humans out of curiosity, but these crocodiles will wait by the river and pounce on any person who may be crazy enough to stand on the banks or swim in the water. Saltwater crocodiles are so aggressive that they attack anything that moves near them. They have been known to take down sharks, tigers, and even elephants.

Chapter Twelve: Boomslang

The first thought that will cross your mind when you see a boomslang is, "Wow! What a pretty snake." Unfortunately, that might also be the last thought that crosses your mind!

Without a doubt, the boomslang is a beautiful snake, especially the young ones that tend to have bright green eyes. This snake is found in many countries throughout Africa, and it loves to hang out in trees as it hunts chameleons, birds, and lizards.

It has a blunt face and big eyes for a snake with such a small head. The males are usually light green in color while female boomslangs are brown. It is a shy snake that rarely attacks any animal it cannot swallow. It is so stealthy that you may not even see it moving on the trees.

Unlike most snakes, the boomslang has fangs at the back of its mouth behind its other teeth. This means that it has to open its mouth very wide (170 degrees) just to inject an animal with its venom. This is one of the reasons why less than ten people have been recorded to have died from boomslang bites.

So here we have a shy, pretty, non-aggressive snake that has teeth at the back of its mouth and has never even killed more than ten people in recorded history. Then why is the Boomslang in this book?

Well, for years, people had assumed that the boomslang was a harmless snake because of the above characteristics. It wasn't until 1957 that snake experts learned just how deadly a boomslang bite could be. The scientist who was handling the snake got bitten, but because everybody thought the boomslang was harmless, he ignored the bite and went on working. He was found dead in his house 24 hours later.

The boomslang has very toxic venom. Once the boomslang bites you, it takes a couple of hours for the venom to kick into action. Some of the symptoms include nausea, headaches, drowsiness, and bleeding in the brain. Without treatment, you will suffer a slow and painful death within three to five days.

The worst thing about the boomslang venom is that it makes you bleed from every orifice in your body. In other words, blood comes out from your nose, eyes, ears, gums, and any other opening that you may have. The venom destroys your red blood cells and internal organs and prevents blood from clotting. You will bleed continually for days and endure a painful death.

The boomslang may not attack a human because the structure of its mouth and fangs is simply not designed for it. However, you do not want to take any chances with this pretty, yet deadly, snake. Most people get bitten when they try to kill or catch the boomslang. If it feels threatened, the snake curls its body into an "S" shape and inflates its neck.

The good thing is that its venom acts slowly, so you have the chance to seek medical attention and get treated with anti-venom.

Chapter Thirteen: Cone Snail

The cone snail is a marine snail that has a beautifully colored shell with unusual patterns and designs. If you were to see one on the seabed, you would be tempted to pick it up. Bad idea!

The cone snail is found along the coral reefs of the Indian and Pacific Oceans. It lives mainly in tropical climates although some cone snails can be found near Southern California, South Africa, and in the Mediterranean Sea. It looks like any ordinary snail and grows to about 12.5 centimeters (5 inches) long.

So, what's the deal with this tiny snail?

The cone snail has a small specialized tooth that it uses like a harpoon. This harpoon contains potent venom that can quickly kill any animal that dares to come near it. The cone snail uses the harpoon to stab small fish and inject its prey with toxins. The venom quickly paralyzes its prey, and the cone snail then swallows it whole.

The harpoon is also very effective against humans. Cone snails have beautiful shells that many beachgoers and divers love to collect. However, large cone snails have harpoons that are big enough to tear through a wetsuit. The venom is a powerful neurotoxin and can easily kill a human being. In fact, a single sting from a cone snail contains enough venom to kill several adults.

Cone snails are very aggressive and are always willing and ready to attack. This makes them extremely dangerous. They are always re-growing their harpoon tooth to ensure they are constantly prepared to strike.

There is currently no medication to neutralize the venom of the cone snail. The only option is to treat the victim's symptoms and keep them alive until the toxins leave their system. It is estimated that 65 percent of the people who get stung by the cone snail and fail to get treatment will die.

People who get stung by this sea creature never even feel any pain. This is because the venom contains a potent painkiller. Pharmaceutical companies are currently conducting more research to determine if cone snail venom can be used to manufacture painkillers.

Luckily for us, cone snails tend to spend most of their time on the seabed where few humans ever reach. Therefore, the number of deaths per year due to cone snails is minimal.

Chapter Fourteen: Hippopotamus

"Hippopotamus" may sound like a friendly name, and the animal itself may look slightly funny, but this is actually the biggest killer on the African continent. No other animal kills more people in Africa than the hippo.

What makes them so dangerous?

Hippos weigh a whopping 3 tons, and only the elephant and white rhino beat it for size. Hippos have large canine teeth that look like tusks. They also have sharp incisor teeth that they use specifically for fighting. The hippo's huge canine teeth may be blunt, but these massive beasts produce the most powerful bite of all the mammals. With a bite force of 1821 pounds per square inch, hippos don't need sharp teeth to do some severe damage to anything or anyone.

Apart from their enormous size and fearsome bite, hippos can also run at a fast pace. They look chubby and slow, especially if you see them wallowing in a pool of water, but this is not an animal you want to engage in a foot race with. Hippos can reach an average speed of 30 kilometers per hour (20 miles per hour).

Another characteristic of hippos is that they simply have a bad attitude. Their extreme aggressiveness makes them very deadly animals, and they will do whatever it takes to defend their territory. Most large mammals usually ignore other animals that aren't a direct threat to them, but the hippo doesn't need to be provoked to attack. They even attack boats that come too close to their territory. This explains why the hippo attacks and kills so many people. They simply charge at you the moment they see you.

The best thing to do when attacked by a hippo is to climb a strong tree quickly. Climbing a frail tree won't help you since the hippo may knock it down using its massive body. If you are lucky enough not to get snapped in half, then you may be trampled to death.

Hippos are herbivores and eat grass and other vegetation. However, there have been reports that hippos have been seen eating crocodiles, wildebeest, and even other hippos. This shows you just how dangerous these animals can be. Even alligators and the mighty crocodile avoid them like the plague.

Chapter Fifteen: Puffer Fish

The pufferfish has a slow and awkward swimming style fish that leaves it vulnerable to attack from predators. However, it comes from a family of fish that have the unique ability to inflate their body when they feel threatened. To get an opportunity to escape from predators, the puffer fish quickly ingests air and water into its extremely elastic stomach. This inflates its size and turns its body into a globe-like shape that scares away any potential predators.

The puffer fish also has tough and prickly skin, and its teeth are fused together to form what looks like a beak. They can be found in the tropical seas off the coast of Japan, the Philippines, and China. Pufferfish grow to a maximum size of 90 centimeters (3 feet) in length, though the majority are usually much smaller. It also goes by the name blowfish and swellfish.

Meeting a puffer fish in the wild can be a dangerous affair. The puffer fish is considered extremely deadly due to the neurotoxin contained in different parts of its body. Its skin, liver, muscle tissue and kidneys are all toxic. This very poisonous fish can kill you if you try to eat it. Any predator that tries to touch a puffer fish will instantly get a taste of its foul-tasting and poisonous skin. In fact, the only vertebrate that carries more venom than the puffer is the golden arrow dart frog.

Even though consuming the puffer fish is a huge risk, this does not stop some people from eating it. The puffer fish is part of the diet of the Japanese people. In Japan, it is called *fugu*, and must only be cooked by special chefs who are trained and licensed. These professionally trained chefs must make sure that they carefully remove the toxic parts of the fish and clean it thoroughly before they cook them. Even so, there have been many accidental deaths caused by eating the puffer fish. Its toxin is 1,200 times deadlier than cyanide.

If you eat a puffer fish that has not been adequately prepared by a trained professional, you will experience symptoms such as dizziness, breathing problems, vomiting, paralysis of the tongue and lips, muscular paralysis, and ultimately, death. Unfortunately, there is still no antidote for this toxin.

Chapter Sixteen: Africanized Honey Bee

Does the name "Killer bee" ring a bell? That's the Africanized honey bee for you. They are small, aggressive, and packed with venom.

Africanized honey bees are a product of the breeding between European honey bees and African honey bees. When European honey bees were taken to South America, they couldn't survive the heat and predators. African honey bees were then imported into Brazil from Africa in 1956 so that they could breed with the European honey bees. The goal was to create a new breed that was gentle yet strong enough to survive the tropical heat of South America.

Unfortunately, some of these African honey bees managed to escape into the Brazilian forests, and they bred with wild European honey bees. The result was the creation of the Africanized honey bees. This new hybrid managed to survive, but they weren't as gentle as everybody expected.

They soon began spreading beyond Brazil and reached Mexico a few years later. Now they can even be found in California.

Contrary to what most people believe, the Africanized honey bee is not as large as the Hollywood movies depict it; it is much smaller than the European honey bee, which also means it packs less venom. Its venom isn't stronger than that of any other type of bee.

So why are they considered deadly creatures?

The Africanized honey bee is super aggressive. When these insects detect any kind of disturbance around their hive, they immediately defend their colony without wasting any time. They attack and sting the perceived threat in such large numbers that they quickly neutralize the threat. The Africanized honey bee will respond to any attack ten times faster and will sting the intruder ten times more than the European honey bee. This is why the Africanized honey bee has caused hundreds of deaths over the last 50 years.

Africanized honey bees know how to adapt to unpredictable environments quickly. They also reproduce very rapidly and can survive on very little nectar and pollen. They can sense danger from a distance of 16.5 meters (50 feet) from their hive. If you come any closer than this, they will attack you. Africanized honey bees are also able to sense vibrations caused by power equipment 33 meters (100 feet) away from the nest. They are known to chase intruders for a distance of 400metres (¼ of a mile) or more.

The lethal dose for an adult human is about 1000 bee stings. If you have an allergic reaction, however, you may die with much fewer stings. The Africanized honey bee will only react aggressively and attack if it feels that the hive is threatened.

Chapter Seventeen: Black Mamba

Of all the snakes that you would ever wish to stay away from, the black mamba should be at the top of your list. The black mamba is found in the eastern and southern parts of the continent of Africa. It is regarded as one of the most venomous snakes on the continent.

Most people think that black mambas are black in color, but that is not true. Black mambas actually have greyish or brown skin, and so the question is, why are they called "black" mambas?

Well, the reason is that the inside part of their mouth is a blue-black color. When a black mamba feels threatened, it opens its mouth and displays this color to warn any predators.

This is one snake that is well-known for its extreme aggression. When a black mamba attacks, it raises its body off the ground, opens its black mouth, and makes a hissing sound. That is usually enough warning to any animal to leave it alone. However, if the animal refuses to get the hint, the snake launches a massive attack.

It doesn't just bite you once or twice. The black mamba delivers several quick bites that inject its toxic venom into its victim. Each bite contains enough venom to kill at least ten people. However, the black mamba only resorts to this kind of extreme aggression when it is cornered. It is a shy snake and will always try to run away when it is confronted.

Interestingly enough, the black mamba's bite is actually quite painless. This deadly snake can bite you once on the finger, and you wouldn't even know it. This is what happened to one South African student who was handling the snake. He never realized that the black mamba he was holding had bitten him, and one hour later, he was dead. Quick and painless! That's how the black mamba rolls . . . or slithers.

Black mambas can grow up to 4.7 meters (14 feet) long and weigh up to 1.6 kilograms (3.5 pounds). Another interesting feature of this snake is its impressive speed. It can slither at a rate of 20 kilometers per hour (12.5 miles per hour). This makes the black mamba the fastest snake in the world!

Chapter Eighteen: Cape Buffalo

Any animal that has such a bad reputation that it is nicknamed "Widowmaker" and "The Black Death" is not something you would want to cross paths with. This is not just another big cow.

The Cape buffalo is found in Africa. There are some buffaloes in Asia that have been domesticated, but the fact that no one has ever managed to put a leash on the Cape buffalo says a lot about its nature. This massive animal is extremely unpredictable, and this makes it too dangerous to be around humans.

The Cape buffalo is a hefty creature that can weigh up to 1,000 kilograms (2,200 pounds). It can grow to a height of 1.8 meters (6 feet). It has humongous and thick horns that span 1 meter (3 feet). It uses these horns to knock just about anything or anyone that stands in its way. It can even gore and kill a lion, and there are times when a Cape buffalo has been seen fighting a white rhino.

When a Cape buffalo gets angry, it begins circling and stalking its prey as it waits for the perfect opportunity to attack. With an average speed of 57 kilometers per hour (35 miles per hour), trying to outrun this colossal beast is not going to work.

Though the Cape buffalo is naturally a bad-tempered animal, it is at its most dangerous when injured. If hunters shoot a Cape buffalo, it runs off and hides in the bushes. The hunters will naturally try to chase down the animal, thinking that they have it cornered. Big mistake! The Cape buffalo knows how to lay a well-timed ambush, and when it sets its sight on its target, it attacks furiously with no mercy. They are also very protective of their young ones and will display outright aggression when one of the calves in the herd is threatened.

The Cape buffalo is responsible for several hundred human deaths every year. However, most of the people who actually get killed by the Cape buffalo are big game hunters. This is an indication of how deadly this animal can be if you try to mess with it.

Now you know why they say, "Nobody survives a Cape buffalo attack."

Chapter Nineteen: Carpet Viper

The carpet viper doesn't usually make the list of most dangerous snakes, but this snake kills around 20,000 people every year. It is also known as the ocellated carpet viper. It inhabits several countries in Africa, such as Kenya, Egypt, Algeria, Sudan, Senegal, and Libya.

Carpet vipers are not large snakes at all. They usually grow up to about 90 centimeters (35 inches) long, and these are the long ones. Short carpet vipers can stretch just a mere 30 centimeters (12 inches). They also tend to move very slowly compared to most other snakes. They have a sidewinding pattern of movement where the upper body stays static while the rest of the body slithers sideways.

These snakes have a head that is shaped like a pear and a body that is kind of chubby. They come in a range of colors and can be yellow, brown, red, or grey with whitish spots all over. These whitish spots look like eyes, and they are meant to confuse any potential predator. As part of its defense mechanism, the carpet viper will rub the scales on its skin to make a sizzling sound. They may be slow movers compared to other snakes, but they are extremely alert.

Carpet vipers spend their days hiding under rocks or shrubs and come out in the evening to hunt. Their main diet consists of spiders, beetles, lizards, birds, mice, and frogs.

With such short, plump bodies and slow speeds, why are carpet vipers even considered as dangerous?

Well, it's all about the number of people who die from its bite. Carpet vipers may not move around much, and they may not be the most venomous snake out there, but they are responsible for killing more people in Africa than any other snake. They are also considered deadly because of the massive damage that their venom does to its victim.

The venom of the carpet viper is slow-acting yet extremely toxic. The toxins in the venom cause swelling near the bite, blistering, extreme pain, and damage to tissues. After 24 hours, the victim experiences internal and external bleeding, as well as organ failure. After a couple of days, the victim's circulatory system simply collapses.

The only way to save the victim is to give them anti-venom as well as blood transfusions. For a carpet viper victim, anti-venom alone just won't work. With the massive bleeding and organs shutting down, adequate medical attention is the only way to survive. Unfortunately, most of the people who get bitten by this snake live in remote and rural areas, and getting a proper blood transfusion can be difficult. For this reason, the carpet viper is regarded to be the deadliest snake in the African savannah.

Chapter Twenty: Mosquito

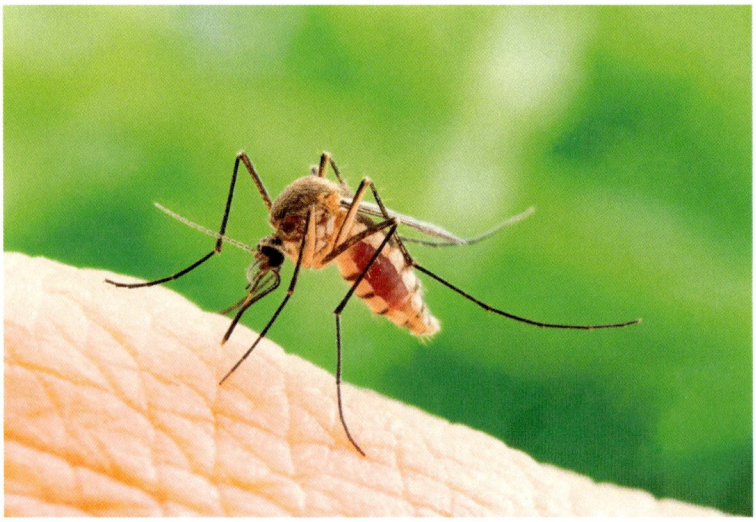

The mosquito is a small insect that can be incredibly annoying. However, this tiny pest is the biggest killer in the entire world.

Mosquitoes can be found almost everywhere in the world, except in Antarctica. The reason it is such a deadly animal is that mosquito bites cause over one million deaths every year. Most of these people die because of a disease called malaria, which is prevalent in Africa. Mosquitoes are so dangerous that they infect between 300 and 500 million people with malaria every year. This is a massive number of people who fall victim to such a small and skinny insect.

This tiny creature doesn't do much damage on its own. It is actually the parasite that it carries that kills people. This malaria parasite is transmitted through a mosquito bite and into a person's bloodstream. However, not every mosquito you see has this malaria parasite. Only the female Anopheles mosquito can spread malaria.

So how is malaria actually transmitted from the mosquito to a person?

When the female Anopheles mosquito bites a person who is infected with malaria, they also suck up the malaria parasite. The mosquito then goes on to bite another person who is healthy. When the mosquito bites the healthy person, the parasite moves into the person's blood and infects them with malaria. Malaria is a disease that is transmitted only through blood, so you cannot get malaria by touching someone. Some of the symptoms of malaria include nausea, fever, chills, and in severe cases, organ failure.

Though malaria can affect anyone, there are some groups of people who are most at risk of dying from this disease. These include pregnant women, young children, and travelers who come from countries that do not have malaria. These people easily succumb to malaria because they have little or no immunity to the disease. Apart from malaria, mosquitoes also spread other deadly diseases like Dengue fever, the West Nile virus, and the Zika virus.

Chapter Twenty-One: Polar Bear

At first glance, polar bears seem like cute and oversized white teddy bears. But as we'll soon find out, these animals aren't very fond of human hugs.

Polar bears are found in the Arctic Circle (North Pole) and love to swim in the icy waters. Their huge paws are slightly webbed, and this explains why they are powerful swimmers. Though they can swim for very long distances, they usually prefer to hitch a ride on floating sheets of ice.

This animal grows to about 2.1 meters (7 feet) tall and can weigh up to a hefty 700 kilograms (1540 pounds). They can survive the freezing weather thanks to the layer of fat on their skin as well as their thick coat of fur. The bottom of a polar bear's paws also has fur to keep them warm and provide a better grip on the ice. Did you know that polar bears actually have black skin? The white coat helps them to blend into their surroundings, but the black skin underneath helps them absorb heat from sunlight.

Polar bears, unlike most other animals, are not afraid of humans. In fact, these are the only animals that will stalk and eat human beings. Other animals may attack humans either to defend their territory or out of curiosity, but polar bears seem to know exactly what they are doing. This behavior may be because they don't get to interact with many humans in their natural habitat. One swipe of a polar bear claw is enough to kill a person. However, incidences of contact between humans and polar bears are rare, so very few deaths are ever recorded.

Polar bears mainly eat seals, and they don't have any natural predators. Male polar bears sometimes eat their own young when they get too hungry. This shows you that polar bears will do anything to survive.

Chapter Twenty-Two: Tsetse Fly

Tsetse flies are true bloodsucking insects. They may look like regular flies, but these particular insects have a taste for blood and nothing else. This is quite unlike the female Anopheles mosquito, which only sucks human blood when it wants to provide nourishment for its developing eggs.

The tsetse fly can be found primarily in sub-Saharan Africa, where it is responsible for transmitting some really nasty diseases. Any human bitten by this insect will develop a condition known as *sleeping sickness*. Animals that are bitten by tsetse flies develop a disease called *nagana*, or *animal trypanosomiasis*.

This fly measures between 7 to 16 mm (0.3 to 0.6 inches) in length. They have a dark brown appearance with dark markings on the abdomen. The male tsetse fly is the one mostly responsible for sucking human blood while the female flies usually prefer larger animals.

The tsetse fly must suck blood every day to survive, and it has developed an extra long mouth (referred to as a proboscis) that can puncture human skin. A tsetse fly can suck up its own weight in blood, which proves just how bloodthirsty this insect is. In the process of sucking blood from humans and animals, the fly collects bacteria and viruses from one victim and transfers it to the next victim. This can easily lead to the spread of many diseases. They usually prefer to prey on people and animals when it is warm outside.

Anyone infected with sleeping sickness will suffer from fever, extreme fatigue, swelling of the brain, and aching joints and muscles. As the disease progresses, the victim develops neurological problems such as personality changes and confusion. Sleeping sickness is such a severe disease that there are areas in Africa where people cannot settle simply because of the large population of tsetse flies.

The tsetse fly has a few other interesting characteristics. For example, the female tsetse fly does not lay eggs. Instead, it has some kind of uterus where it houses and feeds its young ones (maggots) until it is ready to give birth to live larva.

Chapter Twenty-Three: African Elephant

The African elephant is the largest land animal in the world. Its cousin, the Asian elephant, is much smaller in size. The African elephant stands at 4 meters (13 feet) tall and can weigh up to 10 tons. In most cases, the African elephant is gentle and tolerant of humans. However, this giant can quickly turn dangerous and attack without warning.

The African elephant will use its massive size to crush and kill any animal that comes its way, including humans. Adult males often go through periods in their life where they become very aggressive and behave violently. They will even flip over vehicles that get too close to their territory. They are also extremely protective of their young ones and will do everything to protect them.

African elephants are extremely intelligent. Their brain is somewhat like that of a human, and when one elephant dies, the rest of the herd show signs of pain. Elephants sometimes visit the bones of dead elephants and touch them using their trunks. They also have great memories. In one incident in the 1970-80s, villagers killed some elephants to reduce their excess population. A few years later, the young elephants that had been part of the herd that was slaughtered came back and attacked specific villages in what was believed to be a revenge mission.

These animals can be found across the African continent. Since the climate can get quite hot, they have developed extra large ears to release body heat and help keep them cool. If the heat is still too much, the African elephant will use its trunk to suck up some water and spray itself. It will even throw some soil over its back or roll around in mud to apply a protective coat on itself against bugs.

The natural diet of the African elephant is made up of tree bark, fruits, roots, and grass. This animal really knows how to eat, and one elephant can eat as much as 136 kilograms (300 pounds) of food in one day. They have such huge appetites that they rarely even have time for sleeping. African elephants will walk for long distances eating as much as they can just to sustain their extra-large bodies.

Chapter Twenty-Four: Poison Dart Frog

The poison dart frog is one of the most beautiful and brilliantly-colored animals you will ever see. Their natural habitat lies in the tropical forests that stretch from Brazil to Colombia and Costa Rica. Depending on the exact habitat that the frog lives in, its skin bears beautiful designs and brilliant colors such as red, blue, green, gold, yellow, and black. However, no matter how mesmerizing the poison dart frog may look, don't ever try to touch this creature.

This small frog has extremely toxic skin, and the poison dart frog is believed to be the most poisonous animal on the planet. It is essential to understand that there is a difference between poisonous and venomous. A poisonous animal is deadly if you come into contact with its skin or secretions. However, a venomous creature has to bite you and inject the toxin into your body to harm you. Therefore, the poison dart frog is only deadly if it is touched or bitten by any animal.

The color patterns and neon designs on its skin make it stand out from all other species of frogs. The poison dart frog has developed these brilliant hues to warn predators not to come near it. The poison on this frog's skin is ten times more lethal than that of the pufferfish. The deadliest of its kind is the golden poison dart frog, which measures a mere two inches but has enough poison in its vibrant yellow skin to kill ten adult men.

The Embera tribe in Colombia have learned how to make use of the poison in this frog's skin. They use this poison to make poison-tipped darts for the blowguns they use when hunting. This is why this frog is referred to as the poison dart frog.

Many scientists still aren't sure of how the poison dart frog becomes toxic. These frogs survive on a diet of ants, beetles, and termites. Scientists believe that the plants that these small insects eat may contain some poison, and the frog absorbs this poison into its body after feeding on these insects. Funnily enough, it is only wild poison dart frogs that have toxic skin. Those that are raised in captivity never become poisonous, probably because the insects they eat don't come into contact with the same type of wild poisonous plants.

There is research being conducted to explore whether the poison from this frog can be used for medicinal purposes. So far, there are signs that it could be used as a painkiller.

Chapter Twenty-Five: Blue-Ringed Octopus

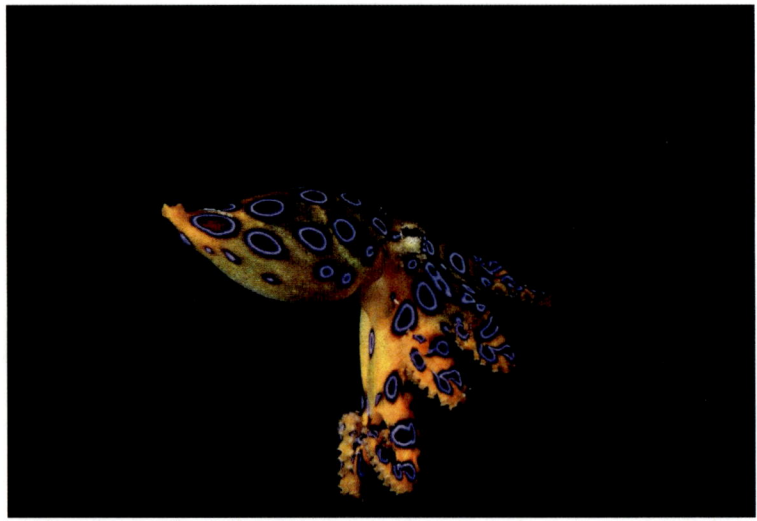

The blue-ringed octopus is a shy and mellow sea creature that loves to hide in rock crevices, waiting for a tasty crab to pass by. It takes advantage of its yellowish-brown skin to camouflage itself among the rocks. It is commonly found off the coast of Australia and in the Indo-Pacific region.

As harmless as this sea creature may look, it is hazardous. When the blue-ringed octopus senses danger, it immediately begins flashing bright blue rings all over its body. This should be enough warning to any predator to watch out. However, if for some reason you don't get the message, this octopus won't launch any vicious attack. It will allow you to pick it up, and while you are mesmerized by its glowing blue rings, it delivers a painless bite using its parrotlike beak.

Most victims aren't even aware that they are in danger. You are just likely to see a small cut with a tiny blood drop oozing out your hand or leg. After about 10 minutes, you begin to realize that something isn't right. Your lips go numb, and speaking becomes difficult. The muscles on your face are paralyzed. Soon enough, you feel nauseous and begin vomiting. Your vision becomes blurry, and all your muscles become weak. Even breathing becomes challenging, and soon, you may lose consciousness. If you do not get treatment quickly, you may die.

The problem with trying to get treatment after a blue-ringed octopus bite is that the doctors might not even know why you are experiencing these symptoms. The cut is so small, and you won't be in any condition to speak and tell them what happened.

The saliva of the blue-ringed octopus contains a very potent venom. This is the same type of venom that the puffer fish has. However, the octopus doesn't make the venom itself. It is believed that certain bacteria in its mouth manufacture the venom. This venom is then spread all over its body. In some cases, the venom of the octopus can be transferred directly via prolonged skin contact. This means that the blue-ringed octopus doesn't even have to bite you to kill you. Touching it can be fatal.

Conclusion

Thank you again for downloading this book!

I hope you enjoyed reading about my book these Deadly Animals. I hope you were able to learn more about a few of the notable species, especially the ones that live quite close to humans. These are amazing creatures still must be respected and appreciated. Best of all, you should learn to stay away from them!

Everybody would know thry should stay away from a Lion, but who would know you should also avoid the harmless looking Cone Snail!

Finally, if you enjoyed this book, please take the time to share your thoughts and **post a review on Amazon**. It'd be greatly appreciated!

Thankyou!

About the Author

Hathai Ross was born in Thailand and then moved to England in late 2004. She has been writing Books for the past 3 years, mainly on Animals which are her passion.

Feel free to contact Hathai at greenslopesdirect@gmail.com

Check out her Amazon profile : Hathai Ross

Next Steps

Please leave me an honest review about the book – I truly value your opinion and thoughts and I will incorporate them into my next book, which is already underway!

Thank you

Check Out My Other Books

Go ahead and check out the other great books I've published!

Snakes: Amazing Facts about Snakes with Pictures for Kids

Dolphins: Amazing Facts about Dolphins with Pictures for Kids

Whales: Amazing Facts about Whales with Pictures for Kids

Sharks: Amazing Facts about Sharks with Pictures for Kids:

Dinosaurs: Amazing Facts & Pictures for Children On These Wonderful Creatures

Ants: Amazing Facts about Ants with Pictures for Kids

Made in United States
Orlando, FL
08 December 2021